The History of Eastbourne

EASTBOURNE is the country's finest example of a planned Victorian seaside resort. Over a century after Brighton and Hastings had been attracting visitors Eastbourne still consisted of an inland village and three seaside hamlets. The town as we know it today is largely the creation of the 7th Duke of Devonshire who had a vision of a seaside resort "built by gentlemen for gentlemen". In 1859 he commissioned a development plan which is still hailed as a masterpiece of town planning. There was a sense of spaciousness and the concept included a one-and-a-half-mile long promenade. To this day the elegance of this original plan shines out.

The Eastbourne area was a wealthy agricultural community in Roman, Saxon and medieval times. The main village of Bourne (now Old Town) was an important market with a fine medieval church. In the late 18th century the idea that sea water was good for the health took hold. At that time the rural area that is now known as Eastbourne consisted of Bourne and the three hamlets of Southbourne (Grove Road), Meads and Sea Houses (Marine Parade). In 1789 George III sent his children to Sea Houses for their summer holidays. By 1841 the total population was only 3,015.

Sea Houses in 1850

At that time the Cavendish and the Gilbert families owned four-fifths of the land and persuaded the London, Brighton and South Coast Railway Company to build a branch line to Eastbourne in 1849. A stagecoach used to take over nine hours to travel from London to Eastbourne whereas the Puffing Billies took two-and-a-half hours.

William Cavendish, the major landowner, became the 7th Duke of Devonshire in 1858. He was keen to develop the natural beauties of Eastbourne and commissioned Henry Currey, a brilliant architect, to draw up a plan for an elegant seaside resort with beautifully laid-out tree-lined boulevards, promenades, elegant squares, terraces, hotels and villas. The central axis was the 80-foot wide **Devonshire Place** leading to the three-tiered **Promenade**. Central control ensured that the villas of the town centre would be in a formal Italianate, classical style with buildings of stucco and slate roofs enriched

with delicate ironwork. Complementary to the Duke's schemes was the Davies-Gilbert development of Upperton, centred around The Avenue with fine squares, avenues and large villas.

Victorian Eastbourne was developed between the Downs and the sea. Between 1871 and 1881 the population doubled to over 20,000. **Eastbourne College** was opened in 1867 and the **Pier** in 1870. In 1872 Currey produced a plan to transform **Meads** into Eastbourne's Belgravia, with mansions of vernacular style, built of red brick, flint and greensand. The Victorian Society considers Meads to be one of the outstanding areas of Victorian architecture in the country.

In 1874 the chapel at **All Saints' Convalescent Hospital** was built. **Devonshire Park** became the cultural centre of the town. A new **Winter Garden** was opened and the Devonshire Park Orchestra was

formed, the first orchestra of symphonic size in any seaside resort. The **Grand Hotel** was opened in 1876 and it was here that Debussy orchestrated *La Mer* and the Palm Court Orchestra later made its name on radio. The **Town Hall** was opened in 1886 to the strains of the *Hallelujah Chorus*.

The Borough Council is active in restoring the beauties of Victorian Eastbourne. While packaged overseas holidays have taken their toll on long stays, Eastbourne is becoming increasingly popular for short-break holidays and day visitors.

The promenade in 1872

The Carpet Gardens

The promenade from the Wish Tower

The pier

Between the Downs and the Sea

EASTBOURNE nestles at the eastern end of the South Downs. It is beautifully positioned, being sheltered by Beachy Head, and has one of the best sunshine records in the country. It has the largest theatre/arts complex outside London, and the marina is the largest composite marina in Europe. It is one of the most popular seaside resorts in Britain and attracts over two million day visitors and almost 600,000 staying visitors every year.

The Downs at Beachy Head

The Town Centre

The town centre essentially consists of broad tree-lined boulevards and quaint squares that were part of the original town plan. The main shopping area is **Terminus Road** which runs from the railway station to the seafront. The Borough Council has recently restored **Sussex Gardens**, a part of Terminus Road, to its Victorian original which resembles a Parisian-style leafy boulevard. **Little Chelsea and Seaside** are other shopping areas. The present magnificent Victorian **Railway Station** was built in 1886 in a mixture of medieval and classical styles, dominated by the fine clock tower and zinc-covered, French pavilion-style roof. It is one of the few Grade II listed railway stations in Britain.

With its distinctive asymmetrical facade and 130-foot (40m) clock tower the **Town Hall** is the most flamboyant and obviously Victorian building in the town. It has a fine Council Chamber.

The **Heritage Centre**, run by the Eastbourne Society, is a delightful example of the flamboyant optimism of so much of Eastbourne's distinctive Victorian architecture. This award-winning Centre illustrates by means of maps, relics, models, photographs, paintings and a video the story of Victorian Eastbourne.

Eastbourne College is one of the country's leading co-educational public schools with over 500 pupils. The Memorial Buildings visible from Grange Road were completed in 1930 and were the result of the munificence of an appeal launched by old boys.

Eastbourne Railway Station

OPEN FOR MORNING
TEA & COFFEE

LUNCHTIME WAITRESS
SERVICE

SAME PRICES AS
NEXT DOOR

RAY HOLLAND

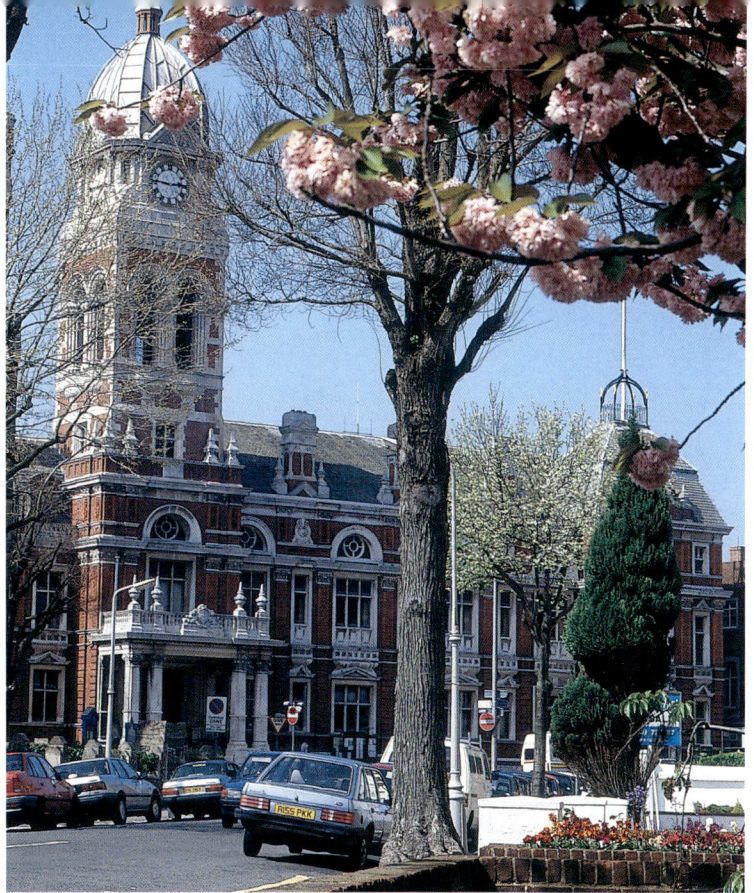
The Town Hall

EASTBOURNE BOROUGH COUNCIL

The French Market

EASTBOURNE BOROUGH COUNCIL

Terminus Road

RAY HOLLAND

Heritage Centre

EASTBOURNE BOROUGH COUNCIL

Eastbourne College

JOHN KEELING

5

The Lamb Inn, one of the oldest hostelries in Britain

Old Eastbourne

Medieval Roots of Old Town

About a mile from the seafront is Old Town, the original village of Bourne. It is a picturesque area steeped in history and old buildings. **St Mary's Church** was erected in the 12th century and has a majestic Norman tower. The Church is connected by a cloister walk to the **Old Parsonage** which used to be Rectory Manor property. It has fine examples of Tudor stonework and is thought to be connected by a secret subterranean passage to a 13th-century vaulted monastic room beneath the **Lamb Inn.**

The Lamb Inn is one of the oldest hostelries in Britain and was the staging post for the London coaches. **Pilgrims**, sitting by the old village centre crossroads and opposite the Lamb in today's Old town, is Eastbourne's oldest house. Believed to have been built by the monks of Lewes Priory as a hostelry on the main road along England's South Coast, its cellars date from the 12th century, its main structure from the late 14th century with both 18th and 19th century additions - it was the solar of a large Wealden hall house, the rest of which disappeared with the construction in the 18th century of Borough House next door. The Guild of the Brotherhood of Jesus, the church body owning it in the 16th century, was forced to sell it at the Reformation to a private speculator - a Catholic recusant had lived here previously, as attested by a coded inscription on one of its beams.

Across the road is the Manor House, formerly the home of The Towner Art Gallery.

Pilgrims

St Mary's Church in 1808

Motcombe Gardens with St Mary's Church Norman tower in the background

Manor Gardens

Hampden Park

Parks & Gardens

There are 200 acres of parks and gardens in Eastbourne, not including the 4,000 acres of the South Downs that lie within the town boundaries. The largest park is **Hampden Park** with mature oaks, lakeside and woodland paths and open spaces.

Gildredge Park is a large open recreation ground. By contrast, **Manor Gardens**, which adjoins the **The Manor House**, has herbaceous borders, hedges, an ornamental pond, a children's maze and contemporary sculpture. **Motcombe Gardens** in Old Town is a quiet, small park around the source of the Bourne Stream from which the town took its name.

There are gardens in profusion, including the **Carpet Gardens, Italian Gardens** and **Helen Gardens.** Eastbourne is the first resort to cultivate a nature park for wildflowers and shrubs that thrive in shingle. This is **Sovereign Park,** east of the Sovereign Centre.

Western Lawns

Horse Show in Gildredge Park

The Manor House from Manor Gardens

Congress Theatre and Conference Centre – Grade II* listed

Devonshire Park Theatre

Winter Garden Theatre

In the Gallery and On the Stage

The largest art gallery and theatre complex outside London.

Devonshire Park has been the cultural centre of the town for over a hundred years and includes the **New Towner Art Gallery** the **Congress** and **Devonshire Park Theatres** and the **Winter Garden**.

The New Towner Art Gallery (Rick Mather Architects) opened in March 2009 and has already been nominated for Global Design and Innovation awards. It is an outstanding example of contemporary architecture and houses the important Eastbourne art collection. It is alongside the Congress Theatre and includes workshops that support artists of all calibre.

The Congress Theatre (D. Westgate and Partners, 1964) was awarded a Grade II★ listing for its special 1960s architecture. It has 1,700 seats and stages orchestral concerts, operas, ballets, international choirs and West End musicals. It is also the setting for conferences.

The Devonshire Park Theatre (H. Currey, 1884; remodelled 1892), sometimes called the "Playhouse", is a beautiful and intimate Grade II listed Victorian theatre which was extensively refurbished in 1903 and again in 1997. It has 900 seats and offers a different play most weeks with pantomime every Christmas season.

The Winter Garden (H. Currey, 1874), also Grade II listed, was influenced by the design of the Crystal Palace. Now that the latter has been lost the Winter Garden is of national importance. It is used for concerts, dance-nights and exhibitions. In Seaside Road stands the **Royal Hippodrome**, known as the Theatre Royal when it was opened in 1883, where summer shows and seaside entertainment are offered.

Evening concerts at the Redoubt Fortress

Along the Prom.

Eastbourne's coastline runs for eight miles from beyond Beachy Head to Sovereign Harbour. The focus of the town is on the Victorian parades – King Edward's Parade, Grand Parade, Marine Parade and Royal Parade – and on the promenade that lies between the parades and the sea.

Starting at the western end is **Holywell Retreat**, steep landscaped cliff gardens tumbling down to a hidden and most beautiful part of the seafront. It was a favourite haunt of King George V and Queen Mary during their stay in 1935. The **Italian Gardens** at the end of Holywell Retreat were built in an old chalk pit. On the cliff top above are the **Helen Gardens** with breathtaking views.

From here to the pier the promenade has three tiers which, when they were built, reflected the three divisions in society, known popularly as "the world, the flesh and the devil". Facing King Edward's and Grand Parades is the majestic sweep of Eastbourne's splendid Victorian hotels, the finest of which is the **Grand** which was designed in 1876. This five-star hotel has just had a multi-million pound refurbishment.

Until the first World War **Western Lawns** were the site of fashionable "Sunday Parades". They now provide the perfect setting for "Airbourne", an annual RAF town show which includes the Red Arrows, and such events as the Classic and Sports Cars Show. The **Wish Tower** (no. 73 out of 74 Martello towers) was built in 1804 as a defence against Napoleon. Eastwards of the **Lifeboat Museum** is the **Bandstand**, built in 1935 and rated the best traditional bandstand in Britain. Screens protect patrons from sea breezes. There is a performance many days in the summer, sometimes featuring military bands.

The **Carpet Gardens** have been a showpiece of the town for over a hundred years and are illuminated at night. The adjoining Victorian **Pier**, constructed in 1870 by Eugenius Birch, is considered to be the finest seaside pier in the country. The promenade continues east of the pier and a new stretch has recently been constructed that extends as far as the Sovereign Harbour.

East of the Pier is the **Redoubt Fortress**, originally built to defend Britain against Napoleon. It now houses a military museum. Some fishermen still bring their vessels ashore near the former lifeboat station. Further along is the **Sovereign Centre**, a swimming pool complex, and, beyond that, the new Sovereign Harbour.

EASTBOURNE BOROUGH COUNCIL

GRAND HOTEL

The Grand Hotel

EASTBOURNE BOROUGH COUNCIL

The Red Arrows at Airbourne

RAY HOLLAND

On the beach

12

The famous 1930s bandstand

On the Water

The largest composite marina in Europe.

Sovereign Harbour Marina

Beachy Head Lighthouse

At the far end of the promenade is the **Sovereign Harbour** which is the largest composite marina in Europe. It is a "locked" marina, accessible 24 hours a day, which accommodates 1,100 vessels. The whole site includes shops and over 2,500 houses, covering 360 acres. Over 4,000 yachtsmen visit the marina every year and it is becoming an increasingly important feature of the town.

For many years visitors to Eastbourne have been able to take a boat trip from the beach adjacent to the pier around the Beachy Head Lighthouse and back. In 1999 there was a severe cliff fall near the lighthouse and the chalk which fell into the sea now prevents the boat from actually going round it. The trip loses little, if anything, from this.

Eastbourne Sovereign Sailing Club races

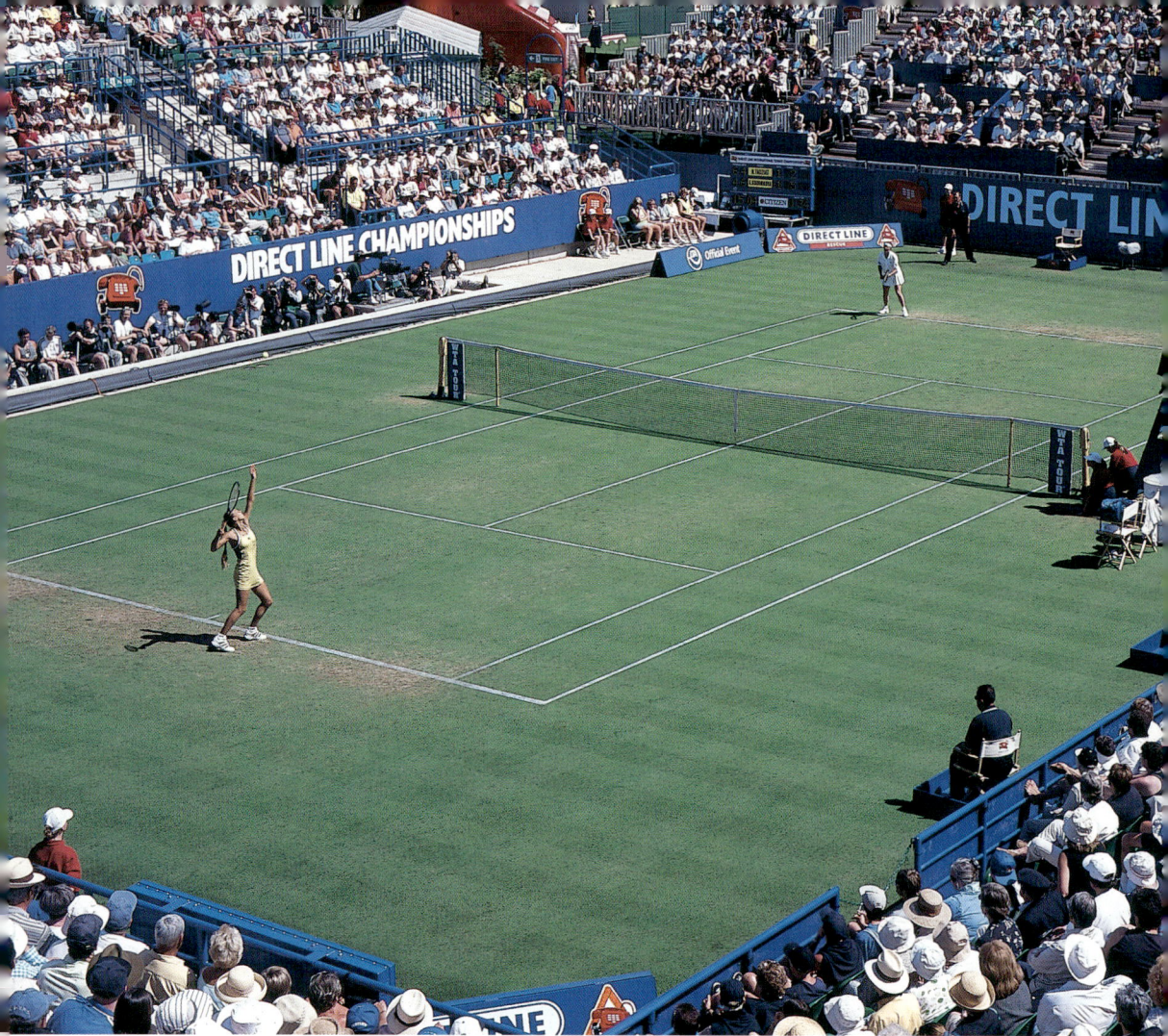

International Tennis at Devonshire Park

Bowls

Sport & Recreation

Eastbourne boasts four golf courses all within striking distance of the town centre. **The Royal Eastbourne Golf Club**, which is over one hundred years old, contains two courses. The Royal, the **Willingdon Golf Club** and the **Downs Golf Club** all offer spectacular views for the discerning golfer. The **Eastbourne Golfing Park** is also available on Lottbridge Drove next to the **Eastbourne Miniature Steam Railway,** which offers endless fun for children and adults alike.

Eastbourne has 60 tennis courts. The **Devonshire Park International Tennis Centre** is world famous because of the Ladies Championship which takes place every year just before Wimbledon. Most of the world's most famous women tennis stars have played on these grass courts and are now joined by a host of male players.

There are many other sports grounds such as the **Saffrons**, where cricket,

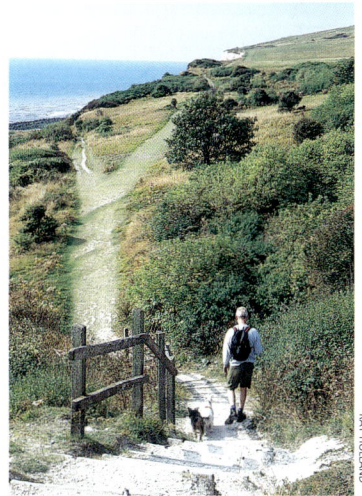

Walking on the Downs at Cow Gap

croquet, football, bowls and hockey are played and a new athletics complex, the **Eastbourne Sports Park,** which opened in 2000 provides an all weather astro pitch and track facilities.

Golf

17

Alfriston market cross – one of the last in Sussex

The Tiger Inn, East Dean

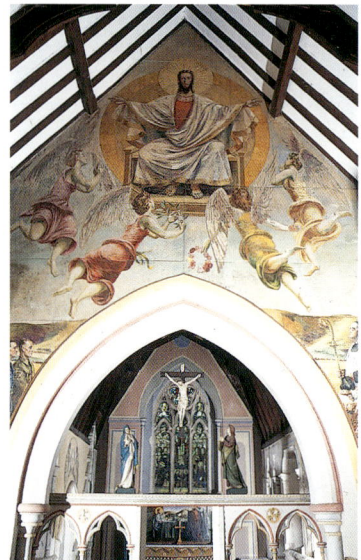

Murals in Berwick Church

Villages

The west side of Eastbourne is bounded by the South Downs. From **Arlington** to the sea is the unspoilt Cuckmere Valley running through a series of pretty villages. **Berwick** boasts a picturesque pub, "The Cricketers" and its beautiful 12th-century church contains unusual murals by Vanessa Bell, Quentin Bell and Duncan Grant, members of the *Bloomsbury Set* who lived at nearby Charleston Farmhouse. **Wilmington** is famous for the **Long Man**, a giant figure 227 feet (69m) tall cut into the turf of Windover Hill. No one is sure when, or by whom, the Long Man was created.

One of the gems of the Cuckmere Valley is **Alfriston** which has been described as the prettiest village in England and is popular with artists. In the village square is one of only two market crosses remaining in Sussex. The Smugglers Inn was once a haunt of smugglers. The George Inn has had an innkeeper's licence since 1397 and the 500-year old Star Inn was used by pilgrims. The 14th-century church of St Andrew is known as the "Cathedral of the Downs". Next to it is the 14th-century thatched and timber-framed Clergy House which became the first

National Trust property in 1891, bought for £10.

Lullington has what is claimed to be the "smallest church in England". Dating from the 13th century it is the chancel of a larger church and has seats for only 20 people. The river passes by enchanting **West Dean** which lies in Friston Forest and thence runs into the sea at Cuckmere Haven. The meanders, now bypassed, and oxbows are the most spectacular in Britain. At the eastern end of Friston Forest lies the village of **East Dean** with its scenic green and Tiger Inn.

Jevington, Litlington and **Alciston** are other pretty villages just to the west of Eastbourne.

North of Eastbourne stretching up to **Burwash** is a hilly farming area dotted with quaint villages and pubs. **Hellingly, Cowbeech, Rushlake Green, Bodle Street Green, Brownbread Street** and **Brightling** are just a few.

There are many vineyards within a few miles of Eastbourne that provide interesting tours.

Friston Church

Historic Buildings

Eastbourne contains 12 conservation areas and 239 listed buildings and the stock of Victorian and Edwardian buildings remains largely unspoilt. **Compton Place** is a Grade I listed building which was originally built in the 16th century as Bourne Place. In the 1720s it was renamed and enlarged. It later became the local home of the Cavendish family and is a fine example of a Georgian mansion.

Classic cars at Filching Manor, Wannock

PAUL FOULKES-HALBARD

Within a few miles of Eastbourne lie a number of interesting historic buildings.

Built during the 15th century, **Herstmonceux Castle** is one of the oldest brick buildings of note still standing in England. With moat, towers, battlements and machicolations it has the appearance of an archetypal medieval castle. It became a ruin in the 18th century but was restored in 1912. In 1948 it became the home of the Royal Greenwich Observatory. In 1960 construction began on the largest telescope of its day which was dismantled and rebuilt when the Observatory moved to the Canary Islands in 1990. The Castle was bought by Dr Alfred Bader who gave it to his old University, Queen's in Kingston, Canada, in recognition of their kindness to him during the war. It is now Queen's International Study Centre. The walled Elizabethan Gardens have been beautifully recreated and are open to the public.

William the Conqueror landed at Pevensey in 1066 and one of his half-brothers built **Pevensey Castle** in the corner of the old Roman fort. It was re-armed in Elizabethan times against the Armada and prepared for defence again during the Second World War.

Michelham Priory is a fine Tudor mansion that incorporates extensive remains of the original Augustinian Priory built in 1229 and also a 14th-century gatehouse. Inside the Priory there are displays of antique furniture, tapestries and paintings. The six acres of gardens encompass a Tudor Barn, a physic garden, a magnificent herbaceous border and a working water-mill.

Filching Manor is a Wealden Hall house built in the 15th century. Within the extensive grounds is a Classic Car Museum containing over 100 historic racing and sports cars, a collection of Bugattis and other rare and interesting exhibits. It also houses Sir Malcolm Campbell's world water-speed record boat, Bluebird K3.

Further afield are **Firle Place**, a Tudor mansion that has remained in the Gage family for 500 years, housing a magnificent collection of porcelain, furniture and paintings; **Charleston Farmhouse** where members of the *Bloomsbury Set* lived for many years; **Bateman's**, a lovely 17th-century house, former home of Rudyard Kipling and now owned by the National Trust; and **Glyndebourne**, with its famous Opera House recently rebuilt by Michael Hopkins.

Pevensey Castle

Herstmonceux Castle

Polegate Windmill

Michelham Priory

The Downs

Since Roman times Eastbourne has been defined by the sea, the marshes on the east and the Downs to the west. The Downs and Beachy Head shelter Eastbourne from south-westerly winds and help to provide it with one of the best sunshine records in the country.

After the First World War there was a real threat of development on the Downs and the Eastbourne Borough Council promoted an Act of Parliament to enable it to compulsorily purchase more than 4,000 acres of Downland, including Beachy Head, for preservation. One of the objects was *"to secure to the public the free and open use of the Downs in perpetuity"*.

that status is now even more assured with the decision to create a South Downs national Park. this measure – embracing 627 sq miles of downland between Eastbourne and Winchester reflects the importance of the south Downs as an Area of Outstanding Natural Beauty and Site of Special Scientific Interest.

Eastbourne's hinterland nurtures a huge range of flora and fauna including some rare species. there are several nature reserves on the Downs. the Seven Sisters centre at Exceat and the Beachy Head Countryside Centre provide and excellent introduction to the area, as well as stunning views of the coast.

Meanders at the mouth of the River Cuckmere

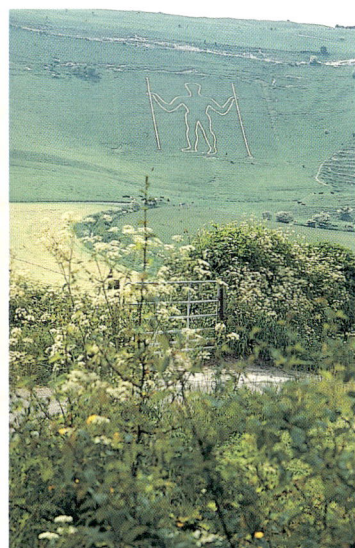

The Long Man of Wilmington

The Downs towards Newhaven

23

Beachy Head

JOHN DARLING

Fishing boat off Beachy Head

Fishing boats on Eastbourne beach

Cliffs & Coastline

The Chalk Cliffs from **Birling Gap** to **Beachy Head** are internationally famous, being the highest sheer cliffs on the south coast. The precipitous cliffs at Beachy Head rise sheer 535 feet (163m) above sea level providing magnificent views. Over one million people visit Beachy Head every year.

Belle Tout Lighthouse, built in 1831 but found to be useless on misty days, is now a private home. In 1999 it was winched back 55 feet (17m) from the eroding cliff edge. It should be safe for sixty years! The present lighthouse built at the foot of the cliffs in 1902 is 142 feet (43m) high and flashes a light every 20 seconds, visible for 16 miles (26 km).

Below Beachy Head are **Falling Sands**, a stretch of golden sands set against the dramatic white cliffs. Access requires descending 100 steps at **Cow Gap**, but the experience is well worth the effort. It is essential to check the tides prior to going down to the beach as retreat to Cow Gap can be cut off at high tide.

To the west of Beachy Head lie Birling Gap, the **Seven Sisters** and **Cuckmere Haven**. Over 600 acres of the Downs with magnificent cliffs belong to the National Trust and the whole area is a paradise for walkers and naturalists.

EASTBOURNE BOROUGH COUNCIL

JOHN COCKER

Birling Gap at sunset

RAY HOLLAND

The Seven Sisters

25

Children's
Eastbourne

Safe bathing at the Sovereign Centre

Part of the seafront east of the Pier is given over to children. **Treasure Island** is an award-winning play centre with an acre of paddling pools, sand-pits, a model Spanish galleon and lighthouse. **Fort Fun** is a two-acre amusement park built like an American frontier fort. Next to it is a children's Go-Kart track. Tranquil **Princes Park** has a boating lake with pedaloes and resident swans. Princess Diana opened the **Sovereign Centre** in 1989. It has a large swimming pool and leisure complex with a fun pool, slides, jacuzzi and a wave machine. There are also competition and diving pools for the serious swimmer. The beautifully laid out **Miniature Steam Railway** in Lottbridge Drove offers nostalgic journeys around Southbourne Lake and includes a nature trail.

Drusillas Zoo Park, to the west of the town, has been voted the best small zoo in the country. With over 400 animals and birds it includes a playground area and railway.

Herstmonceux Science Centre is housed in the old Greenwich Observatory and includes Isaac Newton telescope tours and a collection of hands-on scientific displays. **Newhaven Fort** is a winner with children with its fascinating maze of tunnels and reconstructions of wartime Britain.

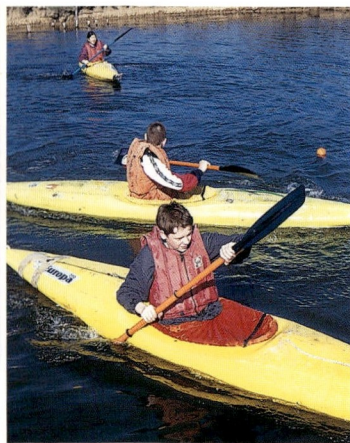

Canoeing on the River Cuckmere

Miniature steam railway

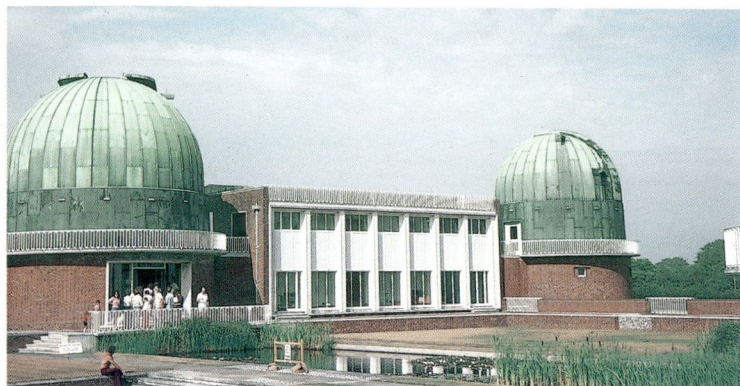

Herstmonceux Science Centre

Drusillas Zoo Park

General Information

A&E	Accident & Emergency Dept
P	Car Parking
	Coach Parking
	First Aid Post
	Lifeguard Beach
	Pedestrian Precinct
PO	Post Office
	Public Conveniences
	Red Cross Centre
i	Tourist Information
	Weather Station

Places of Interest

A	St Mary's Church
B	Heritage Centre
C	Compton Place
D	Town Hall
E	Meads Village
F	Eastbourne College
G	All Saints Hospital
H	Towner Art Gallery

Sports & Leisure

1	Cavendish Sports Centre
2	David Lloyd Leisure
3	Hampden Park Sports Centre
4	The Oval Athletics Track and Football Ground
5	Sovereign Centre

Parks and Gardens

- The Carpet Gardens
- Helen Gardens
- Manor Gardens
- Motcombe Gardens

- Bowling Greens
- Canoeing, Sailing & Windsurfing
- Mini Golf & Putting
- Sailing
- Tennis Courts

Acknowledgements

The Eastbourne Society wishes to gratefully acknowledge the valuable contributions from those named below:

Photographs

Brian Carr
Friends of Devonshire Park Theatre

Mavis Clack
The Eastbourne Society

John Cocker
Eastbourne Photographic Society

Dr John Crook *Winchester*

John Darling *Seaford*

Drusillas Zoo Park *Alfriston*

Eastbourne Borough Council

Eastbourne Sovereign Sailing Club

Paul Foulkes-Halbard
Filching Manor, Wannock

Grand Hotel

Herstmonceux Castle

Ray Holland
The Photocentre, Eastbourne

John Keeling FBIPP
Poyntington, Dorset

David Sellman *Pembury, Kent*

Sovereign Harbour Marina Ltd

John Stanley FRPS
Eastbourne Photographic Society

Malcolm Woolley
Cornfield Studios, Eastbourne